Power of a Woman Series

CLAIM *Your*

Luci Brigit Rani Marisol Tracy

INHERITANCE

Dr. Cassundra White-Elliott

This is a work of fiction combined with the Word of God. Any resemblance to actual occurrences is purely coincidental. Included scripture are from the Holy Bible, primarily King James Version, except where noted.

CLF Publishing, LLC.
www.clfpublishing.org

Copyright © 2018 by Cassundra White-Elliott. All rights reserved. No portion of this book may be reproduced, stored in a retrieval system, or transmitted by any form or any means electronically, photocopied, recorded, or any other except for brief quotations in printed reviews, without the prior permission of the publisher.

Cover design by Senir Design. Contact information: info@senirdesign.com.

ISBN # 978-1-945102-33-2

Printed in the United States of America.

Introduction

Regardless of the road upon which you travel during your lifetime, whether you are rich or poor, young or old, male or female, educated or not, Black, White, yellow, or brown, there will always come a time or two when you will be faced with a challenge. Psalm 34:19 states, *"Many are the afflictions of the righteous: but the Lord delivereth him out of them all."* Therefore, our heavenly father knows we will endure afflictions. But, He has a plan for us.

Moreover, in Luke 10:19, Jesus says, *"Behold, I give unto you power to tread on serpents and scorpions, and over all the power of the enemy: and nothing shall by any means hurt you."* There are times in our life when the enemy (Satan) will rear his ugly head to wreak havoc. John 10:10 informs us, *"The thief cometh not, but for to steal, and to kill, and to destroy: I am come that they might have life, and that they might have it more abundantly."* Jesus came and died on Calvary's cross to give us an abundant life. And, upon His death, Satan became a defeated foe. And although Satan has yet to be rendered inoperable, we have victory in Jesus who is alive and well, reigning in heaven with His father Jehovah.

Although many believers are aware of the verses mentioned above, they do not exercise the power that is rightly theirs as children of the Most High God, the one true living god. They fail to utilize their voice and instead remain silent, allowing the enemy to take what is rightfully theirs. That, my friends, is not the will of God.

Romans 8:31-39 clears up all doubt about God's position as it involves our victory in times of adversity. *"What shall we then say to these things? If God be for us, who can be against us? He that spared not his own Son, but delivered him up for us all, how shall he not with him also freely give us all things? Who shall lay any thing to the charge of God's elect? It is God that justifieth. Who is he that condemneth? It is Christ that died, yea rather, that is risen again, who is even at the right hand of God, who also maketh intercession for us. Who shall separate us from the love of Christ? shall tribulation, or distress, or persecution, or famine, or nakedness, or peril, or sword? As it is written, For thy sake we are killed all the day long; we are accounted as sheep for the slaughter. Nay, in all these things we are more than conquerors through him that loved us. For I am persuaded, that neither death, nor life, nor angels, nor principalities, nor powers, nor things present, nor things to come, Nor height, nor depth, nor any other creature, shall be able to separate us from the love of God, which is in Christ Jesus our Lord."*

Let's move forward to the task at hand. Read Numbers 27:1-11. *"The daughters of Zelophehad son of Hepher, the son of Gilead, the son of Makir, the son of Manasseh, belonged to the clans of Manasseh son of Joseph. The names of the daughters were Mahlah, Noah, Hoglah, Milkah and Tirzah. They came forward and stood before Moses, Eleazar the priest, the leaders and the whole assembly at the entrance to the tent of meeting and said, "Our father died in the wilderness. He was not among Korah's followers, who banded together against the Lord, but he died for his own sin and left no sons. Why should our father's name disappear from his clan because he had no son? Give us property among our father's relatives." So Moses brought their case before the Lord, and the Lord said to him, "What Zelophehad's daughters are saying is right. You must certainly give them property as an inheritance among their father's relatives and give their father's inheritance to them. "Say to the Israelites, 'If a man dies and leaves no son, give his inheritance to his daughter. If he has no daughter, give his inheritance to his brothers. If he has no brothers, give his inheritance to his father's brothers. If his father had no brothers, give his inheritance to the nearest relative in his clan, that he may possess it. This is to have the force of law for the Israelites, as the Lord commanded Moses'"* (NIV).

Zelophehad, a descendant of the tribe of Manasseh (one of the half tribes of Joseph, son of Jacob), had died. As a member of one of the twelve tribes, Zelophehad was guaranteed a land inheritance when he and his family reached Caanan. However, prior to the Israelites leaving the wilderness and sojourning into the Promise Land, Zelophehad died. At that time, it was Israelite custom for an inheritance to pass from father to son. If there were no son, the inheritance would pass to a brother. If there were no brother, the inheritance would pass to the deceased man's father's brother (his uncle).

Upon Zelophehad's passing, he left no sons. However, he did leave five daughters: Mahlah, Noah, Hoglah, Milkah and Tirzah. And, his daughters were concerned about the transfer of the father's land, believing it should rightfully pass to them as his offspring. At that time, Moses was the chief leader, so the daughters took their case to him and the other leaders, having faith justice would prevail. After hearing the details of the case, Moses, wanting to do what was right in the eyes of the Lord, decided it would be best to consult God on the matter.

After receiving instruction from the Lord, Moses returned to the five daughters. According to God's instruction, Moses allocated the land that would have gone to Zelophehad to his daughters. From that point forward, Israelite tradition was changed.

Not only did Zelophehad's daughters have faith in God, but they used their God-given authority to speak, voicing their opinions and expressing their concern. They did not permit the current laws to deter them from gaining what should be rightfully theirs. In doing so, they also exercised courage. After all, II Timothy 1:7 says, *"For God hath not given us the spirit of fear; but of power, and of love, and of a sound mind."*

Using the example of these five courageous women, we (women and men) can gain motivation to exercise our rights in situations we face where our rights are being denied. In the midst of a male-driven society, these women banded together for one cause. In our personal situations, we may not have anyone standing with us or fighting by our side as Zelophehad's daughters did, but with God on our side, how can we fail? Romans 8:31b declares: "*If God* be *for us, who* can be *against us*?"

Furthermore, I John 4:4 states, *"Ye are of God, little children, and have overcome them: because greater is he that is in you, than he that is in the world."* And, Romans 8:37 says, *"Nay, in all these things we are more than conquerors through him that loved us."* Allow these verses to encourage you when you find yourself alone physically and you are faced with a trial. Remember, spiritually you are never alone. God is forever with you.

To claim your inheritance or that which is rightfully yours, using the following steps may prove helpful.

Step One- Pray for God's Instruction/Direction

Psalms 37:23 says, *"The steps of a good man are ordered by the LORD: and he delighteth in his way."* You never want to make a misstep or lose valuable time by being untimely, making unwise choices, or going in the wrong direction. Proverbs 3:7 says, *"Be not wise in thine own eyes: fear the LORD, and depart from evil."* Sometimes, we don't know what to do or how to go about doing what we do know. So, getting directions from God is the wisest choice we can make. James 1:5 says, *"If any of you lack wisdom, let him ask of God, that giveth to all men liberally, and upbraideth not; and it shall be given him."* Life does not come with an instruction manual, and we oftentimes lack the necessary wisdom to navigate through our trial. But, God will provide us with wisdom if we ask Him.

After conversing with the heavenly father, and obtaining much needed direction, instead of being fueled by fury, a sense of entitlement, or even fear, we can move to Step Two with confidence and a plan of action. After all, Habakkuk 2:2 instructs us to write the vision and make it plain.

Step Two- Know Your Legal Rights

To be certain of your legal rights, you may want to consult a lawyer, whether it is a probate attorney, family law attorney, or a labor law attorney. Just be sure the lawyer specializes in the proper area of law that meets your needs. Prior to consulting with the lawyer, make a list of questions you need answered, so your consultation is most fruitful.

Step Three- File Forms

File forms with the court, if necessary, and document as much as you can, showing why you believe you have a right to the property in question or to show how your rights have been violated. The more information you provide, the more ammunition you add to your case. When filing forms, being minimalistic is <u>not</u> the key. In this instance, more is definitely better.

Step Four: Gather Evidence

While waiting to appear before a judge, if necessary, prepare and gather as much evidence that will support your position of what you are fighting for. When the time comes, present the information in an orderly, systematic fashion. Also, review the court documents you submitted prior to appearing in court, especially if it has been a while since you filed, because the judge will refer to them.

Step Five- Await the Outcome

This may be the most difficult step, but it is a necessary one. Do not rush the process. Believe God is working on your behalf. Philippians 4:6-7 says, *"Do not be anxious about anything, but in every situation, by prayer and petition, with thanksgiving, present your requests to God. And the peace of God, which transcends all understanding, will guard your hearts and your minds in Christ Jesus"* (NIV). Patience is one of the nine fruit of the spirit. Exercising patience may be difficult during that trying time, but it, along with the eight other fruit, will prove beneficial to you.

Going through the aforementioned stages may assist in providing you a victory in the trial you are facing. However, we would all do well to remember our victory is in the hands of the Lord, and we should receive instruction/direction from God and not go our own way. Meanwhile, God protects us from the hands of the enemy.

"He thwarts the plans of the crafty, so that their hands achieve no success" (Job 5:12). We must also remember every desire we have may not be the Lord's will. If that is the case, it may not come to pass. However, if something is rightfully ours or our rights are somehow violated, the Lord is fully on our side to ensure everything the devil stole from us is restored (Proverbs 6:31).

In all trials, we must trust the Lord with our whole heart, exercising faith. With our faith, we can move mountains from our path. Matthew 17:20 says, *"And Jesus said unto them, Because of your unbelief: for verily I say unto you, If ye have faith as a grain of mustard seed, ye shall say unto this mountain, Remove hence to yonder place; and it shall remove; and nothing shall be impossible unto you."*

Read the following five accounts of individuals who endured trials and life-changing circumstances. From their situations, you will better understand obtaining a victory is no easy feat. But, *"… with God nothing shall be impossible"* (Luke 1:37).

Luci Lee

Most entrepreneurs begin developing their business sense at a young age. That was certainly true of the Murdock brothers, and Stan Murdock led the pack of three. They were inseparable. Well, as an inseparable as they could be being one year apart. Stan was the oldest, followed one year by Mike, and Pete followed one year behind Mike. Their entrepreneurial adventures began in junior high school and continued right into senior high.

When Stan was in eighth grade, he noticed a girl selling candy from her locker and from her backpack. He loved candy as much as the next kid, but he hated melted chocolate. Trying to eat a candy bar that had melted was not worth the struggle in his opinion.

As he watched his peer sell candy day after day, he noticed she would have a wad of one-dollar bills along with pockets of loose change. His mind wandered to all he could do with some extra pocket cash. That day after school, as he walked home with Mike, who was in seventh grade, he began to discuss selling candy ideas with him.

By the time the two brothers arrived home, they had come up with the brilliant idea of selling boxes of hard candy. First, it would not melt, and second, they were everyone's favorite candies. The next weekend, they purchased boxes of Grape Heads, Apple Heads, Lemon Heads, and Cherry Heads. Then, they emptied all the boxes of candy into a very large bowl and mixed the flavors together. Then, they redistributed the mixture into each of the original boxes.

The plan was to explain to their customers that they would have the best of all worlds in just one box, regardless of which box they chose. While the customers enjoyed the medley of flavors, the two brothers enjoyed the money that poured in, even sharing a little with Pete who was still at the elementary school.

Each box of candy was purchased for $.10, but with all four flavors in one box, the duo sold them for $.25 each, turning a profit of $.15 per box. In most cases, each customer bought four boxes surrendering a full dollar at one time. At first, the duo could hardly keep up with the demand. Quickly, they learned about supply and demand.

From that point to the end of the school year, the duo sold boxes and boxes of their sweet treats. At the start of the next school year, Stan moved into ninth grade, Mike elevated to eighth grade, and the duo evolved into a trio when Pete came to their school as a seventh grader. The Murdock team of three was then complete.

With Pete on the team, the inventory increased with his idea to add gum. Stan's idea was to have one product and do it well like In-and-Out Burger. He didn't want to get lost in the shuffle by not having a specific product for someone. That was how the entire idea of mixing flavors came about. They didn't want fellow students requesting grape or cherry and then having to dig through their backpack looking for a specific flavor. That would waste time and draw attention from teachers and other school authorities. They wanted to keep suspicion to a minimum, especially because selling goods on school grounds was not permissible.

Pete understood Stan's logic, but he convinced his two brothers by letting them know even In-and-Out Burger had a few other products, such as French fries and a small variety of drinks to go along with the burgers. After a lengthy discussion, both Stan and Mike agreed to Pete's idea. To keep things simple and easy, Stan and Mike kept the candy in their backpacks, and Pete housed the gum.

That routine stayed with them from junior high until they graduated from senior high. Then, each of them went to college to study business and earn a bachelor's degree, each with a different focus within the field of business. They began to discuss more seriously the idea of starting a business of their own. Finally, they settled on a candy business but on a larger scale, of course.

They spoke with their parents about their desires, and the first question their parents asked was whether they wanted to redistribute candy from other companies or create their own brand. Unanimously, the three young men answered, "Our own brand." The next step was to get someone to create a few different types of candies and to hire a packaging firm and one to market.

From the onset of the idea and launching the first few candies in the mid-70s to the celebration of forty years in business, the company's sales had been very lucrative. Some of the Murdock success was due to their marketing manager, Luci Lee.

Luci was in her early 50s now, but she had worked with the company since she was hired twenty-four years ago. So, she had worked there for literally half her life. Pete had heard of her marketing expertise from a friend of his who had hired the firm she worked for to promote the launching of a new product his company had developed. Upon his friend's recommendation, Pete also hired the same firm for one particular product but was so pleased with Luci's creative ingenuity that he hired the same firm for three future projects. Each time, Luci led the marketing team, and thus, the product was a success.

After reviewing the revenue increase after each ad campaign, Pete discussed with his brothers his desire to bring Luci to their business full-time. Stan and Mike took note of how many billable hours they spent hiring the firm versus how much it would cost to have Luci on their payroll. Offering her a competitive salary would be far less expensive than the cost they had been incurring.

Once the brothers agreed to invite Luci to their company, they had the Human Resources Department send an official employment offer to Luci Lee by courier, and the sealed envelope had to be signed for by Luci herself. Luci responded to The Murdock Company immediately to thank them for the offer. She asked for some time to think about it before responding. They consented. When Luci placed a second call to The Murdock Company, she requested a meeting. Upon granting her request, a date and time were set.

Luci was excited yet nervous about the meeting and the opportunity to head up the marketing department. During the course of developing advertisement and marketing strategies for The Murdock Company, she had met all three of the Murdocks at one time or another. On the day of her meeting, she had no idea which of the three she would be meeting with, if any. When the receptionist guided her to Conference Room West, she was surprised to see all three Murdock brothers seated at the table. Her anxiety grew as she shook each of their hands prior to taking the seat they offered her.

After the pleasantries were exchanged, the Murdock brothers went into detail about each project Luci Lee had worked on and how her creativity and insight contributed to the company's candies being known near and far. Luci smiled at their accolades, as she nodded her head and said, "Thank you." The brothers took the meeting as a positive sign.

Stan took the lead and asked Luci if their offer of employment interested her and if so, were the terms satisfactory. Luci said she was definitely interested, but she had a concern about her compensation. She explained when she initially received the offer, she thought it was fair as it was comparable to her present salary at the marketing firm. However, her present employer somehow learned of the Murdock offer and offered Luci a raise to stay on with them.

The brothers knew that meant they needed to enter a bidding war to gain the prize: Luci. However, rather than go through the theatrics, Mike removed a slip of paper from his legal pad and asked Luci to write a figure that would seal the deal to bring her to The Murdock Company. Luci nodded, but she ignored the sheet of paper. She reached into her leather binder and pulled out three sheets of paper that held typed information. She slid one sheet over to each of the Murdock brothers.

After looking at the amounts typed on the paper and the additional criteria concerning vacations and freelance work, the brothers looked at each other, communicating only with their eyes. Stan spoke to Luci, stating her times were agreeable. She smiled with glee. All four of them traded handshakes. Pete asked Luci how soon she could start. She stated she needed to give the firm ninety days, so she could finish all projects she was currently working on.

Three months later, Luci joined The Murdock Company and was excited about the new adventure in her career. Due to her familiarity with the Murdocks' expectations, the transition was very smooth.

For the next twenty years, Luci and the Murdocks worked in concert, promoting new candies added to the inventory as well as former candies to ensure continued sales. However, one day tragedy struck, changing the dynamics of The Murdock Company.

One weekend, Mike, his wife, and children took a mini vacation to the Colorado Rockies to ski. Skiing was one of Mike's favorite pastimes, other than sampling new candy recipes. Mike believed skiing was a great way for his family to bond. After two days of enjoying the fresh new snow, the family was lounging around the fireplace when Mike's wife noticed there were not enough supplies to make Smore's. One of their teenage sons offered to go to the local market. Having reservations about a relatively new driver driving on icy roads, Mike declined his son's offer and took the drive himself.

On the way to the market, an antelope darted across the road, causing Mike to jerk the steering wheel to the left. The ice on the road caused the tires to spin around in a continuous circle. Just when Mike thought the car was about to stop moving, another car rounded the same blind curve he had just come around and hit him directly in the driver side door. The impact caused his car to quickly slide across the ice and ram into a tree. A low branch penetrated the front windshield. A large piece of glass fell inside the car and went inside Mike's chest, piercing his heart. Before the ambulance could arrive, the vital organ shut down, refusing to pump blood throughout the body.

When the news reached his family and brothers, a great loss was experienced. His wife was then a widow, and his children were fatherless. The Triple Murdock Brothers, as they were affectionately known during their high school years and from then on, became the Duo Murdock Brothers, but no one called them that aloud. Having been in business side by side for over three decades, Stan and Pete not only grieved the loss of their brother but of their business partner. For them, The Murdock Company would never be the same.

Nevertheless, Stan and Pete carried on with business as usual - as best they could. They divided Mike's responsibilities and added them to their own. Their faithful staff, in all departments, knew exactly what to do, and they worked diligently whether the bosses were there or not.

Just when the new routine became customary, another unexpected change occurred, shifting the business foundation once again. Approximately two and a half years, after Mike's untimely demise, Stan died in his sleep. The autopsy revealed he had suffered a massive heart attack. Immediately, Pete began to experience severe depression due to the unexpected loss of his two older brothers. His parents were yet alive, but they were elderly – in their late 80s. He was in his early 60s.

For the next year or so, the employees rarely saw Pete. When he did work, he worked from home. As a result, the company's revenue began to decline. The profit and loss margin was not too wide at first, but over time, the margin increased. It was time for Pete to make an executive decision - before the company he and his brothers had worked so hard to build folded.

After thinking long and hard about it for about three months, he decided it would be best to downsize the business in order to keep it afloat. That would mean determining which employees stayed on and which were to be let go. Before deciding which employees would fall into one of the two categories, Pete decided whoever fell into the "pink slip" category would receive a severance package, and that package would depend upon the length of time the individual had worked for the company.

Over the next week, Pete compiled two lists, after reviewing the performance, length of employment, salary, and expertise of each employee. The next Friday, before the close of business, Pete called twenty-seven of the sixty-four employees into his office, one by one, to let them know they would no longer be working for the company after that day. He thanked each of them for their service and handed them their severance package.

To her surprise, Luci Lee was one of the employees who received the notice and a severance package. To say the least, Luci was devastated. At that point, she had been employed by the Murdock company just shy of twenty-five years, the time it would qualify her to receive her full pension. Although she had not yet completed the required paperwork, she would be eligible for retirement in three months.

As Luci sat at her desk, placing her items into the box that had been placed there while she was meeting with Pete, tears fell from her eyes in a continuous stream. So many thoughts clouded her mind, such as her oldest son having one more year of college. When her children were teenagers, she and her husband had promised them if they went to college and passed all classes each semester, they would not be required to work and their parents would cover all educational and personal expenses. She didn't know how she would explain to her husband she no longer had an income to contribute to the household or college funds.

Normally, in a situation like that, a person would begin to search for another job. But, Luci was not naive. She knew the chances of her finding a position in her field at her age would be hard to do. To solidify her belief, she learned her assistant, who was twenty years her junior, had retained her position while Luci had been let go.

Over the weekend, Luci shared her experience with close friends and family. Most had the same non-verbal reaction and audible response. However, one shared a bit of advice. When Luci mentioned her thoughts of hiring an attorney, her friend thought it was a good idea but offered another solution instead, but agreed if his solution did not pan out positively, then Luci should definitely consult an attorney. His suggestion was to call Mr. Pete Murdock and request a meeting with him to plead her case regarding full retirement. Her friend stated she had nothing to lose by asking. On the other hand, she had everything to lose by going to court unnecessarily – time and money.

Luci took her friend's advice and called The Murdock Company the next Monday morning. The operator transferred the call to Pete's office, and his secretary answered. Luci promptly requested an appointment with him. The soonest his secretary could schedule her was on Wednesday, two days later. Luci accepted the appointment.

Over the next two days, Luci typed a list of reasons why she should be granted her full pension. At the same time, Pete was compiling a list of reasons why he would not give Luci her job back. Both were ready with a caseload of ammunition to present to the other and was confident about their position. However, it was rather heartbreaking for both of them that their professional relationship had come to a close in that manner.

On the day of the meeting, Luci walked into Pete's office with a tear-stained face, but she was deter-mined to stand her ground and not shed a tear while doing so. He welcomed her in and asked her to take a seat. Then, without giving her a chance to speak, he promptly started his discourse, listing several reasons why he could not give her job back. On the top of his list was her failure to educate herself about the growing trends in marketing and advertising, including new technologies. He stated he noticed over the last few years, Susan, her assistant, was primarily responsible for the new designs. Then, he stated that the primary reason for making all cuts was due to decreased revenue.

After listening to all Pete had to say without interrupting, Luci waited until he invited her to speak. Very calmly, Luci informed Pete she had not come to request her job back. A look of surprise covered his face. Then, he apologized for his assumption. Next, he asked why she had come if not to request reinstatement. Luci informed him she wanted to request her full pension as she was only three months shy of earning it, having worked twenty-four years and nine months.

Pete's head fell backwards and a roaring laugh bellowed from his mouth. His response shocked Luci, and tears sprang from her eyes. She could not understand what was funny about her situation or request. Wiping her tears away, she forced herself to wait patiently while Pete's hysterics died down. About a minute later, Pete calmed himself and look intently at Luci.

To her surprise, he began to apologize for the oversight, explaining how pressured and overwhelmed he felt. He told Luci he would definitely grant her request because the pension was rightfully hers. Then, as he had done when he met her the Friday before, he thanked her for all her years of service with The Murdock Company.

Moments later, Luci left The Murdock Company for what would probably be her final time. A smile covered her face and joy filled her heart as she pulled out her cell phone to call her husband and share the good fortune. He was happy to hear Luci's report and was thankful they had not shared the news of the layoff with their children.

Having Luci's pension as additional income, similar to her regular paycheck, all expenses, including college tuition, would be manageable.

Now, instead of looking for a job, Luci was going into full retirement. The following month, her husband and sons held a celebration in her honor!

Brigit

In May 2012, just eight months after the horrific tragedy of 9/11 took place on United States soil, Brigit moved from Paris, France to Long Island, New York. At fifty-eight years of age, Brigit had experienced the brutal murder of her husband of twenty-eight years. Six months later, after settling the estate that belonged to her and her husband and saying a temporary goodbye to her only child – a son – she boarded a plane.

After being in the States for only nine months, she met and eventually fell in love with Enrique Vasquez. Although her heart yet longed for her deceased husband and she missed him every day, she knew she had found true love again for the second time in her life. She was uncertain what the future held for herself and Enrique, but she believed he was a rare gem – an honest, down-to-earth gentleman, who showed nothing to her except respect, love, and appreciation. However, to anyone looking from the outside of the relationship, Enrique and Brigit must have certainly looked like an odd couple who was mistakenly matched together. That sentiment was definitely held by Enrique's adult children.

Enrique was sixty-nine years old, and due to the hard work and tremendous efforts he had placed into building his own company from the ground up in its formative years, his age was readily apparent upon his face and in his body. His gait was a little slower than most others his age, and his once stark black hair had peppered. On the other hand, his wit and humor were still as strong and formidable as ever. His cultural background was Guatemalan, and as a result of good eating at the hands of his wife and their in-house cook, he always managed to be a little on the healthy side. To add to his somewhat physical challenges, he only stood 5'9", which made him short for a man.

Brigit, eleven years Enrique's junior, was very astute in business, holding several advanced degrees in marketing and advertising. If one were to watch her walk across a crowded room, he would question her name and position because she moved with authority and grace, as do most French people. While keeping her hair the color of a natural blonde, Brigit had worked hard over the years to keep her weight to a minimum, her figure slim, and her skin smooth, taut, and youthful. Although it is widely known those of European descent tend to age more rapidly than other cultures, Brigit was somehow able to defy those odds. Maybe she had genes similar to those of Cindy Crawford. And, she stood 5'10" tall – an entire noticeable inch over Enrique. Then, when her feet were adorned with her standard three-inch heels, she towered four inches over him.

So, based solely on the physical appearance of the two individuals, no one would have anticipated the development of a love relationship. Nevertheless, one sprung to life, and they both welcomed the opportunity to cultivate it.

From the onset of their father's engagement to Brigit, which occurred only a few months after they had begun dating, all three of Enrique's children questioned their father's behavior, which they considered hasty, and Brigit's motives, which they considered questionable. Enrique was outraged by his offsprings' blatant disrespect toward his future wife.

He and their mother had gone to great lengths to raise them to be respectful adults, and as far as Enrique was aware, he and his late wife had been successful. In an effort to quell their growing tempers and frustrations, Enrique met with them and sternly rebuked their behavior. At the same time, he listened intently to their concerns. Afterward, he continued to stand his ground, moving forward and developing his relationship with Brigit.

Despite Enrique's attempts to satisfy his children's concerns regarding Brigit and his engagement to the sudden stranger who appeared in his life not long after her arrival to the States from overseas, Emilia, Enrique's eldest child, decided to take matters into her own hands, without her father knowing, of course.

Emilia hired a private investigator to delve into the specifics of Brigit's husband's death. She was aware he had been murdered, but she speculated about whether or not foul play was involved and if Brigit were the catalyst of the foul play. Prior to hiring the private investigator, Emilia had invited Brigit to lunch, giving the impression that she wanted to get to know Brigit better. However, her motive was to learn more about the unsolved murder of Brigit's husband.

As they dined at the restaurant Scarpetta Beach, on scallops with black truffles, peas, and Aleppo pepper with a Caesar salad, they made small talk. Emilia learned more about Julian, Brigit's son, and she shared with Brigit small tidbits about her husband Alejandro, whom Brigit had met on a few occasions.

Once Emilia believed she had warmed Brigit up enough, she tactfully questioned her about the events surrounding her husband's murder. Her efforts were to no avail because Brigit burst into tears, and that brought Emilia's questioning to an immediate halt. Respectfully, Emilia backed off, but she instantly finalized her decision to hire a private investigator to gain the desired answers in a more private and hopefully more lucrative manner.

After the initial consultation, where she expressed her desires to the private investigator, Emilia waited for nearly three weeks before she was able to receive a full report. Then quite unexpectedly, on a Thursday afternoon, one hour before her normal lunch break, Emilia received the long-anticipated text message from Mark, the private investigator. He wanted to set up a meeting at her convenience. Emilia was anxious to learn all Mark had discovered, and she was tempted to leave work immediately to meet with him. However, wisdom prevailed. She did not want to cause any red flags to go up and draw concern from her boss with an abrupt change in her work etiquette. Therefore, she remained at work until the end of the business day.

At 5:15 that same evening, Emilia pulled her brand-new Tesla coupe into the parking garage of the building where Mark's office was located. After a few moments of waiting for the elevator and then going up twelve floors, she hurried down the corridor to Mark's office. Finding the door ajar, she knocked briefly and entered.

Mark had already informed her that his secretary departed daily at 4:30pm, and he would be in his office just beyond the secretary's desk. Because it would be difficult to hear her knocking, he had told her to simply enter the outer office and go directly to his. Following Mark's instructions, Emilia went to his office, greeted him, and took a seat.

Mark slid an envelope across his desk to Emilia. Without words, she emptied the contents onto his desk and began reading carefully, while intermittently looking at photographs. The long and short of it was Brigit's husband had been brutally murdered, and although the spouse usually sits at the top of the suspect list, Brigit was quickly eliminated. As a matter fact, she had never been formally charged.

In December 2011, while most people were busy going from one store to the next, checking names and gifts off their list, Pierre, Brigit's husband, was in his office after hours. The company's Christmas party was scheduled for the next evening, and Pierre was responsible for printing bonus checks and preparing the hefty gift cards and certificates for the raffle.

Each year, the company raffled off gift cards and gift certificates to the employees. The gift cards held amounts from $250 upwards to $1000. The gift certificates were all for trips to other countries for a vacation getaway, usually for a family of four.

Word had gotten out around town, and somehow word had gotten into the wrong ears. As Pierre placed the gift cards and certificates in separate envelopes adorned with winning numbers on the outside, two men wearing ski masks suddenly appeared in his office without warning and without a sound. Before Pierre realized his office have been intruded, the first man was upon him with a knife sliding across Pierre's jugular vein. Pierre had expired before his corpse hit the desk.

Later that night, the security guard noticed a light on underneath Pierre's office door. After knocking several times, the guard opened the door and called into the spacious office. Having received no response, the guard entered and discovered Pierre's body slumped upon the desk on the top of blood-stained envelopes. The guard checked for a pulse and immediately dialed 911.

After the body was removed, the authorities began their investigation. They were able to ascertain there were two assailants. However, they were never able to confirm their identities, only their motive, which was theft. The assailants wanted the gift cards and certificates for the trips, probably to sell later. The total value of the stolen merchandise was approximately $100,000.

When Emilia received the results from the private investigator, she was not completely relieved when she learned Brigit's husband was the victim of a robbery that was in progress when he stayed late at work. She had been certain she would find something sketchy or questionable about his murder. However, that was not the case. The investigator's findings should have placed Emilia's mind and growing suspicions at rest, but they did not. She felt in her gut that Brigit had an ulterior motive, and she believed it involved her father's wealth.

Enrique was a self-made millionaire. In his young adulthood, he worked for a distribution company. The first two years, he was enthused to be working and putting money into his pocket. Opening his own business was the furthest thing from his mind. After beginning to date seriously, Enrique wondered how he would ever be able to afford to care for a wife and children.

Eventually, his mindset shifted, and he began learning the various components of the operation by closely watching the details of how each department was run. All he was unable to witness firsthand, he had to speculate and put two and two together in order to have complete understanding of the business operations.

Another six years went by, during which Enrique saved to acquire the necessary start-up capital for his business because he did not desire to get a business loan. Finally, with great excitement, Enrique launched his business, and after fifteen years of working long hours, while his wife raised their three children almost single-handedly, he landed the contract of a lifetime, one any business would be grateful to receive. With that contract, Enrique's company earned its first million dollars over the next two years. From that point forward, Enrique and his family were set for life.

His wife did not have to worry over the monthly household bills any longer. He did not have to worry if he would make payroll for his employees. Their children did not have to worry if their parents would be able to afford to send them to college. When the time came, they were able to attend the college of their choice – as long as their grades were up to par – because a low GPA was not an option for attending an ivy league or prestigious school.

After two of Enrique's children who had elected to go to college and had graduated, they became successful in their careers and started families of their own. The third and youngest child elected to join her father's staff and forgo attending college. In her own right, she became just as successful as her two older siblings. Unlike them, she had no family of her own, so she had no one to be accountable to besides herself.

Then suddenly without warning, a month after celebrating their thirty-second wedding anniversary, Enrique's wife fell ill. Six months later, she succumbed to her illness, causing their family of ten (with spouses and children) to decrease by one. Enrique, his children, and grandchildren were all taken by storm; they were devastated.

At that time, Enrique's youngest daughter, Evaline, who worked at his company, moved out of her loft and back home with her father. Because he was approaching seventy years old, she was concerned about him living alone although he was not completely alone because he had a cook and a housekeeper who were both at his residence in the Hamptons five and sometimes six days a week, keeping the meals coming and the 10,000 square-foot mansion in immaculate condition.

A year and a half after his wife's untimely death, Evaline noticed her father's daily routine changing more and more each week. When she had first moved in, a driver would transport them both to the office in the morning and back home at the end of the day. Little by little, that had changed. Enrique began to insist on driving himself or calling a car later in the morning.

Evaline's first thought was her father was beginning to slow down either due to depression from missing his wife or either due to his age. She even wondered if he was experiencing health challenges of his own. Thus, she insisted he visit his physician. Of course, she tagged along, so she could hear firsthand any concerns his doctor may have had, so she could report back to her siblings. The last thing they wanted was to be blindsided again as it had been with the news of their mother's health condition.

Hearing the doctor give her father a clean bill of health, Evaline breathed a sigh of relief. However, she had yet to understand her father's change in office hours and not to mention his late nights. But, all became clear when he introduced Brigit to his children.

Despite his children's readily apparent objections, Enrique and Brigit were wed only five months after introductions had been made. Then…

Four years and three months later, Enrique suffered a massive heart attack and died. Once again, Brigit suffered heartache from the loss of her husband.

After the memorial service for Enrique Vasquez was over and the probate process was completed, his adult children, their spouses, and Brigit sat alongside a table in the family home, waiting intently for Enrique's will to be read. Everyone knew Enrique had changed his will approximately a year after he married Brigit. However, he had not shared the specifics with his children, to keep controversy and complaints to a minimum.

On several occasions, in the first two years of their marriage, Brigit had argued against Enrique making changes to his will on her behalf because she had done quite well for herself in business, and Pierre had left her well-to-do financially with his substantial life insurance policy. As time carried on, Brigit learned more about her husband. She began to understand clearly that he was a man who took care of his own, especially the woman to whom he was married. It was not in him to do otherwise.

At the table, Brigit, her three stepchildren, and their spouses sat quietly. (Evaline had married by that time.) The eerie quiet almost made the executor of the will nervous to read it aloud. He could tell the tension in the room was very thick. He observed the active participants very closely. Brigit sat very stiff backed as she fiddled with her fingers. Both daughters constantly ran their fingers through their hair, a trait inherited from their mother. The son tugged at his beard off and on. The three spouses attempted to calm their mates, but their attempts appeared futile.

Finally, Matthew, the executor, spoke. It was his duty to inform each party what had been gifted by Enrique. Typically, those who stood to inherit some-thing from a deceased party are apprised beforehand of exactly what they can expect. However, in that case, the unveiling would be a complete surprise as per Enrique's instructions.

Near the beginning of the reading, smiles could be seen appearing on each of the children's faces. Enrique Jr. smiled when he heard he inherited thirty-five percent of all of his father's cash assets, stocks, bonds, and investments. The same went to Emilia, who smiled as well, as she grabbed and squeezed her brother's hand, who sat to the left of her.

Evaline inherited the family business and all future profits, while being named CEO with complete governing power, and twenty percent of all her father's cash assets, stocks, bonds, and investments. Each of the children seemed pleased with their share of their father's estate. However, all of their smiles turned upside down when Brigit's name was called.

As Matthew read her portion of the inheritance, fists were formed and slammed down on the table. No one worried too much when they learned she had been gifted ten percent of their father's estate, until they learned the estate was valued just below $100 million. Understanding ten percent of one hundred million is ten million, they grew livid.

Their angst grew even more when Brigit was also given the family home, the home which all three of them had grown up in from the time they were teenagers to the time they had moved out on their own. That was the home their mother had raised them in and with Brigit now being the new owner, they felt part of their heritage was being stripped away.

Before the meeting came to a close, Enrique Jr. openly contested Brigit's inheritance. Matthew had forms ready for just that occurrence and handed them over to him. Enrique passed the forms to his wife, and she began filling in the required sections.

The level of cordiality that had been developed over the past five years was extremely low and was then greatly diminished after the reading. The rejection hurt Brigit, but she refused to allow the negative emotions to consume her. She took the legal hit from the children and was determined to stand her ground. She accepted the reading of the will and her inheritance for just what it was – and gift from her husband from beyond the grave. She had not wanted the family home. She would have been content to purchase a home for herself elsewhere. But, she respected her husband's final desire for her.

Until the children's concerns were addressed, the estate was tied up. During that period of time, Brigit was called to several depositions where she had to state her case. She was asked about her financial state prior to marrying Enrique. She was questioned about her former husband's death. She was asked how she and Enrique met and about their courtship. She was required to submit bank statements and tax returns. Time after time, she felt her privacy was being invaded.

Each time Brigit received a request to appear before a judge or mediator, her heart sank further and further. Eventually, a dear friend of hers insisted she visit her physician for fear that Brigit was going into an irreversible depression. At one point, Brigit did not want to answer any more questions or submit any-more paperwork. She had had enough. The same friend encouraged her to hang in there and not to throw in the towel. She told Brigit, "This inheritance is rightfully yours. Claim it!" Brigit blinked back tears and breathed a deep breath. Brigit didn't know if she could pull it off, but her friend reminded her of all she had experienced over the years and how she had made it through. Her friend told her the battle was almost over and to hang in there.

That night, Brigit took a sleep aid, so she could be well rested for yet another meeting the next morning. After sleeping soundly for six hours, she rose the next morning and prepared a light breakfast. After eating, showering, and dressing, Brigit drove to the deposition. Remembering to breathe deeply, slowly, and calmly, she arrived ten minutes early. To retain her sanity, she did not go in right away. She did not want to run into Enrique's children and allow their disposition to ruin hers.

Right at 9:02am, just on the deposition was due to begin, Brigit walked in and took her seat. With no further delay, the results of the children's complaint were read.

Brigit was awarded everything her husband had left to her. Nothing was reversed. She walked out with her head held high and joy in her heart. Her husband's final wishes for all his family members had been honored. Inside, Brigit rejoiced as she dabbed the tears from her eyes.

Rani

One Saturday evening, Rani sat cross legged on her bed, enjoying her favorite pastime – web surfing. Instead of hanging out at the local club like most 18 and 19-year-olds, trying to land their next hook up, Rani preferred the solitude and serenity of her home, particularly her bedroom.

Of all the sites Rani surveyed, she especially loved those that shared interesting facts and pictures of art and antiques of all kinds. In the midst of performing random searches, Rani came across a YouTube video. Someone had captured bits and pieces of a jewelry auction he had attended while vacationing in Florence, Italy. The pieces of jewelry exhibited for auction were exquisite and timeless.

As Rani watched, she became more and more mesmerized because the auctioneer shared the historical background for each piece along with the fair market value. Most of the jewelry was valued well over ten million dollars for each piece or set (necklace and earrings or necklace and bracelet). The auctioneer explained the high values were due to each piece of jewelry being crafted from rare gems and diamonds of the highest quality. Furthermore, if the jewelry had belonged to a person of royal blood or paraded around by a notable person, the value increased substantially.

During the video presentation, Rani began to get sleepy. Normally, she would simply close her laptop without stopping the video and go to sleep. That time, however, she wanted to see the remainder of the presentation, so she decided to bookmark the site. That way, she could retrieve the video easily to continue viewing it. Just as she lifted her finger to set the bookmark, a necklace appeared on the screen. It looked vaguely familiar, but Rani could not recall where she had seen it. She continued listening to see if someone famous had worn it. Unfortunately, no one's name was mentioned. Rani thought maybe her mind was playing tricks on her. So, she decided to call it a night to get some rest before her college classes the next morning.

The next day, Rani navigated through her regular routines of breakfast, classes, lunch, and her part-time job. Throughout the day, her thoughts constantly returned to the necklace in the video. With each thought, she was becoming more certain she had seen the necklace somewhere before.

When Rani returned home, she found her mother in the kitchen preparing dinner while video chatting with her sister who lives in another state. Rani hugged and kissed her mother and blew kisses to her aunt. Then, Rani took the stairs to her bedroom. After tossing her backpack on the chair and removing her shoes, she jumped onto her bed, pulling her laptop onto her lap. Immediately, she went back to the video of the jewelry auction. She hit the reverse button, moving the video back to just before the necklace was shown. Then, she enlarged the video to full screen. The necklace appeared.

Rani jumped off the bed, leaving the laptop behind. She did not bother to push pause either. She ran down the stairs, passed her mother in the kitchen, and moved into the living room. Her mother asked where the fire was, but Rani failed to answer.

Standing in front of the fireplace, Rani found what she was looking for. Above the mantle was a painting of Rani's great grandparents, her mother's grand-parents. Around Nana's neck was the same necklace that had been exhibited in the auction. Well, it appeared to be the same to Rani. To verify, Rani raced back upstairs to grab her laptop, wondering why she had not brought it downstairs with her. *Too late now*, she thought.

Once Rani had made it back downstairs to the kitchen, she asked her mother to step into the living room with her. Without knowing the reason, her mother obliged, telling her sister she would call her back later. With her laptop open and the video cued to the necklace, Rani quickly and briefly explained. Her mother nodded without saying a word. Rani pushed play, and they both watched the necklace being auctioned along with a bracelet that was mentioned but never shown. At the end of the auction, simultaneously, they lifted their heads to view the painting. Rani's mother gasped. Her reaction let Rani know they shared the same thoughts.

Then, Rani asked if her mother knew who had painted the portrait and why he would add such expensive pieces of jewelry to it. Before her mother answered Rani's question, she quietly pointed to the bracelet her grandmother had on her wrist. It was a match to the necklace. Without verbal communication, both women looked at Nana's ears. However, Nana's earrings were not a match.

As her mother stood quietly, Rani re-asked her the question about the artist. In lieu of a direct answer, her mother simply shook her head. Rani took her mother's nonverbal communication to mean she did not know why the artist would choose to add the jewelry in. But tears began to develop in the corners of her mother's eyes. Rani placed the laptop down on the sofa and took her mother into her arms. At that moment, Rani knew there was more to the story.

Releasing herself from Rani's arms, her mother walked away quietly. Then, after a few steps, she told Rani to wait there and she would be right back. After what seemed to be a great while to Rani, her mother returned with an envelope. She handed it to Rani who quickly pulled the contents free. It was a set of six photos and some documents. Some photos contained Nana, and others were of Nana and Papa. In each photo, the necklace could be seen hanging around Nana's neck. Rani gasped.

Her mother then explained that the artist had not added the necklace and bracelet in because Nana was actually wearing them during the photo shoot, and the painting was made from the photo many years later. She further explained that the jewelry were family heirlooms that had been passed down several generations until they had reached Nana. Nana was planning to pass the necklace to her only daughter, Rani's mother's mother, but there was a fire. Rani had heard about the fire on many occasions before.

In 1918, one late summer night, a fire broke out at the house of Sylvester (Papa) and Earnestine (Nana). The elderly couple was consumed by the fire, along with all their earthly possessions. At that time, they did not permit Blacks to have safety deposit boxes at banks, so all valuables were stored in the family home. After their unrecognizable corpses were buried, the family searched the ruins of the family home, but the jewelry and other valuables were never recovered.

At one time, arson was suspected, to cover up the theft of the valuables, but it could never be proven. Also, the jewelry was never insured, so the family had never been compensated for the loss. Over time, the family moved on, taking the missing items as a loss, having no hope of ever recovering them.

After Rani heard her mother share the horrific experience, she was internally enraged. All the injustices her people had suffered at the hands of those in power before she was born and even in present day infuriated her. She grew more and more adamant to dig into the past and come up with answers. Then, just as quickly as the idea had entered into her mind another one came along to replace it. She thought it would be wiser to follow the jewelry by finding out who had purchased it at the auction and go from there.

After making several inquiries and hitting road-blocks, seven months later, Rani achieved a viable lead that helped her get on the right trail. All other leads had run cold, but the newest lead led her directly to Beverly Hills. Rani secured a plane ticket and into the friendly skies she went.

As Rani sat aboard the 747 Boeing jet, she replayed the events of the last seven months, from the time she suspected her great grandmother's necklace was alive and well to the time she boarded the aircraft. First, she reviewed the YouTube video to attempt to gain the name of the company who had hosted the auction. Then, she contacted the company in search of information on the auction for that particular date, which she also gained from the video. Making the call, Rani was told someone who worked the auction would call her back. That call did not come in for a week.

When Rani received the call, the woman on the other end informed her the jewelry had not been sold. Rani breathed a sigh of relief, only to feel a bit of stress return when the woman told her the jewelry was no longer in the possession of the auction company, for it had been transferred from overseas to a facility in the States. That gave Rani some comfort, knowing it was closer to her than she anticipated. That company was hosting a jewelry auction in California. Rani requested the contact information for the organization to be sent to her by email. The company representative consented.

Once Rani received the requested information, she followed the same procedure as she had with the first company. However, her attempts were unfruitful. Unlike the first company, the representative was reluctant to provide information on the necklace and bracelet, stating it would be a breach of contract with the owner. When Rani told the representative she suspected her family was actually the true and original owner of the jewelry, silence fell on the other end of the phone. Rani had to ask twice if the representative was still on the call before she received an answer. Finally, the representative told her to take the matter up with the proper authorities.

Taking the advice given, Rani began to contact several agencies in California, following her family lawyer's lead. Finally, one agency agreed to look into the matter but only after Rani provided what she believed was proof of ownership. With the documentation Rani provided, the agency contacted the auction company, and that was the official start of their investigation.

After a couple of weeks, the agency informed Rani their attempts at identifying the jewelry were positive, but a jewelry expert needed to check the necklace and bracelet for authenticity. That, of course, was an additional fee. Retaining the agency's assistance had been costly, but Rani had not requested the financial assistance of her parents. Having the necklace and bracelet returned to her family was something Rani wanted to do for them, particularly for her mother who was the rightful heir now that her own mother was deceased. Rani's great grandmother would have passed the necklace to Rani's grandmother who would have then passed it to Rani's mother.

However, the fee for the jeweler to authenticate the jewelry would take the last of Rani's saving, which wasn't much, but it was all she had. Reluctantly, she placed a call to her older brother Tyrone. Rani had been keeping Tyrone and their parents abreast of the advancements in the recovery of the family heirlooms. Listening to his sister, Tyrone could hear tension increase in Rani's voice as she began to discuss the financial component. Tyrone abruptly cut his younger sister off in the middle of her monologue, asking her how much she had spent to date and if there were outstanding expenses that needed to be covered. Rani knew beating around the bush would just be a waste of time, so she did not belabor the point. She answered her brother's questions.

Once she was done, Tyrone told her he would pay for the authentication fee and for their airline tickets to California. Rani noticed how smoothly Tyrone had invited himself on the trip out west with her. She smiled to herself, as she knew he just wanted to help bring that chapter to a swift close. From his perspective, over half a year was too long to be on a scavenger hunt. In that case though, he knew the journey was well worth each and every effort his sister had placed into it.

As Rani and Tyrone sat quietly on the plane, Rani wondered how long they would need to be in Beverly Hills and if they would be taking the necklace and bracelet home with them. Tyrone, on the other hand, had his mind on his pregnant wife and his job. His wife was due to have their first child in less than a month. During the entire pregnancy, Tyrone had not been away from her at any point, and he had loved enjoying the entire pregnancy experience with her. As far as his job was concerned, it really wasn't a good time to take off, but he did not want Rani running around the west coast alone, plus he wanted to be able to cover any expenses that may have arisen while they were there.

Rani was thankful to have Tyrone by her side. He really was an added comfort as her stomach was a ball of nerves. During the entire process, she had been strong and determined. Once she was on the cusp of the finality of her efforts, she was more nervous than she had ever been in her entire life. She desperately hoped everything panned out in her family's favor, and she knew she would be devastated if things went awry. She had sparked hope within her mother, and Rani did not want to disappoint her.

After Rani and Tyrone landed, obtained a rental car, and had checked into their hotel rooms, they decided they should eat before retiring for the night. Neither of them really wanted to go too far, so they opted for the hotel restaurant. The next day at noon, they headed to Beverly Hills for their one o'clock appointment. The jeweler was scheduled to meet them where the jewelry was being held to both authenticate and verify the identity of the pieces. Both Rani and Tyrone were nervous about the outcome, but both were hopeful.

When Rani and Tyrone arrived to the location the jewelry was being housed, they were ushered into a private vault to wait for the jeweler to arrive. No more than ten minutes later, an elderly man with a slightly balding scalp was brought into the vault. He extended his hand first to Rani and then to Tyrone, introducing himself as George, the jeweler. George then took a seat at the table across from them on which he placed a kit of tools.

Claim Your Inheritance

As George removed the necessary tools from his kit, someone brought a light in and placed it on the table. Rani and Tyrone exchanged glances as they watched the jeweler prepare for the task that lay ahead. Not wanting to interrupt his flow or thought pattern, they remained quiet. Then, a representative entered the vault with a shatterproof glass box that housed the necklace and bracelet. He had a set of keys in his hand, swinging gently. Directly behind him was another attendant who also jingled a set of keys.

After placing the glass box on the table next to the jeweler, one attendant placed his key in one of the two locks and turned. The second attendant placed her key in the second lock and turned. The top of the box opened, and the first attendant lifted the necklace and bracelet out and placed them on the jeweler's cloth. Seeing the jewels sparkle, Rani let out a long gasp and clutched her chest. Tyrone looked on quietly in amazement.

George sprang into action, with the light shining on the jewels and his magnifying glass sitting in his eye socket. It took him nearly ninety minutes to survey all the gems, one by one, as well as the 24-karat gold that served as the base for the necklace. Once the jewels had been authenticated, George asked Rani for the certificate of authenticity, which included the numbers of the original jeweler's stamp of identification.

Turning each piece over, George verified the tiny, barely visible numbers that were listed on the certificate. He turned off the light, removed his magnifying glass from his eye, and looked at Rani and Tyrone and then at the two representatives. "The necklace and bracelet are matches to those listed on the certificate of authenticity." The representatives nodded their heads, and one requested the proof of purchase from Rani. She produced the copy she had acquired during her research. The representatives exited the room without a word. Again, Rani and Tyrone exchanged glances.

After waiting twenty minutes in silence, the two representatives re-entered the vault. One representative thanked the jeweler for his time and the verification. The second representative spoke to Rani and Tyrone. She explained how the actual company came to possess the necklace and bracelet. It was a transfer from the original auction company in whose care the owner had placed the jewelry. Then, Rani and Tyrone were informed that the proof of legal ownership from the supposed owner had been falsified. However, the company had not let on their awareness to the supposed owner. Instead, the owner had been called to come to the company to collect the jewelry.

Rani was surprised to hear the last bit of information and was about to interrupt to ask why the necklace and bracelet would be returned to the supposed owner. The representative saw the look on Rani's face and lifted her hand to stop Rani's interruption. She explained when the supposed owner arrived the next day at 9am, the local authorities would be there to make an arrest. At that bit of news, both Rani and Tyrone sighed a breath of relief and leaned into each other with a collective smile.

The next day, Rani and Tyrone returned to the auction company at 10am to take possession of their family's heirlooms. The jewelry was presented to them in the same shatter-proof glass case along with the keys. All legal documents plus the new document of authenticity from George had been given to Rani the day before.

When Tyrone made the travel plans to return home, he and Rani decided to delay informing their mother of the good news. Rani would simply place the exquisite jewelry into their mother's hand while Tyrone captured the look on her face with a timeless video.

Marisol and Juan

It was Valentine's Day, and like a world full of other couples, Marisol and Juan would be celebrating the day of love with dinner at a four-star restaurant. Unlike the other times Marisol had dined with her boyfriend, that day she was very nervous. It wasn't as though they had not celebrated Valentine's Day before, for they had been together for six years by then. No, Marisol was nervous because she had a big surprise for Juan, and she wasn't quite sure what his reaction would be.

As Marisol searched through her expansive closet for something to wear that evening, she took out one outfit after another just to return them all back. Feeling frustrated and dissatisfied, Marisol sat on her bed and stared blankly into her closet. Finally, she remembered the new blue sleeveless evening dress she had purchased a month ago. *Perfect*, she thought. Everyone else would most likely be wearing red or black, so blue would be perfect, so she would not blend into the crowd. She wanted to remain the center of Juan's attention.

An hour later, Juan knocked on Marisol's apartment door. He was always on time, and Marisol certainly appreciated that quality about him. Her smile was wide and broad as she walked to the door to let him in. Juan glanced over to the dining room table and admired the bouquet of roses he had sent by special delivery earlier that day.

The bouquet consisted of white roses, red roses, and yellow roses. They were simply beautiful. Marisol loved the array of colors, and the florist had arranged them perfectly. When Marisol saw Juan eyeing the vase of roses with a sly yet pleased smile on his face, her smile grew even wider, as she threw her arms around his neck and squeezed him tightly. She whispered into his ear, telling him she had something for him, too. However, she elected to wait until they got to the restaurant. Not expecting a gift from her, Juan simply nodded his head.

Once they made it to the restaurant and had been seated at their table, Juan reached across the table to hold Marisol's hand. Without words, they told each other how much love they held in their hearts for one another with only a touch of the hand and a look into each other's eyes. As the gaze lingered on, Marisol could not hold her anticipation much longer. She was about to burst at the seams. Just then, the waiter walked over to take their drink order. Juan took the liberty of ordering a nice bottle of champagne to celebrate their evening. The waiter nodded at Juan's choice of champagne and proceeded to fill their water glasses with chilled sparkling water. When the waiter walked away, Marisol reached into her oversize hand-bag and pulled out a gift wrapped with gold paper and a gold bow and handed it to Juan.

Juan was surprised but pleased to receive a gift from his girlfriend. It wasn't that she was not accustomed to giving him gifts, but he always saw Valentine's Day as an opportunity for men to show women how much they cared for them. He knew he should not be trapped into society's way of thinking because love does flow both ways, but that was simply the mindset he had developed over the years.

Carefully, Juan unwrapped the package, which to him appeared to be the size of a picture frame. Once the wrapping was removed, he saw he was correct because there was a frame inside. But as he looked in expectation for the image, he was surprised to see there was no image inside the frame. Instead, it was a letter on a doctor's letterhead. Reading carefully, he noticed it was the results of a pregnancy test. One word stood out: POSITIVE. Slowly, he looked up from the test results and across the table to Marisol, who was holding her breath. Without words, he stood from his seat and went to her side of the table, lifted her from her seat and hugged her tightly.

As Juan hugged Marisol, the tears of joy flowed from their eyes. They had discussed having children, but neither one of them had expected to begin the nine-month process at that point. They both had thought it would be planned. Juan released Marisol from his bear hug and kissed her gently on the lips. Right then, the waiter returned with the bottle of champagne and was preparing to uncork it. Responding quickly, Juan stopped him, told him the good news, and asked him to replace the champagne with a bottle of sparkling apple cider. The waiter smiled, congratulated the happy couple, and took the champagne bottle away. The couple retook their seats and dried their eyes.

After ordering their meals, they each picked up their glass of apple cider and prepared to toast. Juan told Marisol how happy he was about them starting a family together. Marisol told Juan she could not have found a better man with which to have a family. Juan told Marisol to drink the entire glass of apple cider instead of taking a sip. She didn't understand his reasoning, but she went along with his suggestion as she watched him finish his glass in one long gulp. She attempted to do the same, but to her surprise something fell from her glass into her mouth. Quickly, she removed the item and looked at him very confusedly. In her hand, she found a sparkling diamond ring.

Before she could question Juan or say one word, he was down on his knee next to her chair, taking her free hand into his. He proposed. With a loud scream and a new set of tears, she leaped from her chair and into his arms. While they were both kneeling down on the floor, with the entire restaurant watching them, Marisol screamed over and over, "Yes! Yes!" The crowd applauded loudly, matching the couples' excitement. Somewhat embarrassed, the couple stood to their feet, hugged tightly, and kissed briefly before taking their seats.

Seven and a half months later, Marisol gave birth to a 7 lb. 6 oz. baby boy whom she and Juan named Juan Jr.

Six months after their son was born, they shared their nuptials in a public display with over three hundred guests in attendance. Aside from the day their son was born, Marisol and Juan agreed their wedding day was the happiest day of their lives.

About a year and a half later, the couple gave birth to another son whom they named Marco.

Then, like with all couples, trouble hit. Unable to find common ground, through the art of communication, Juan and Marisol found themselves fighting about every little thing, from finances, to raising their children, to who was cooking dinner, and everything in between. Eventually, the arguments escalated, and Marisol and Juan were unable to resolve their differences. So, they decided to divorce after six years of marriage for their own sanity and the mental and emotional stability of their children, having a full understanding it would be an adjustment for all involved parties as well as some damage being sustained.

Juan thought it would be best for him to leave the family home, leaving Marisol and the children to remain in their familiar environment. He knew the breakup would cause a disruption to the children's regular routine, so leaving them in their own rooms and in the care of their mother seemed like the best option at that time. Meanwhile, Juan found an apartment for himself that had an extra bedroom, so the children could come over at any time and feel as though they were at home in the father's home and not like strangers or visitors.

After a few months of shuffling the boys back and forth between the two homes, Marisol grew tired of the shuffle and decided to go to court to gain full custody of the two children, so she could have a set visitation schedule for Juan. Juan didn't take kindly to being dragged into court. However, he obeyed every court order established for him and his family.

After much mediation and standing and sitting before court officials on numerous occasions, Juan and Marisol were awarded joint custody of the children, with Marisol being the custodial parent. Both parties were content with that arrangement although it had been Marisol's desire to have full rights over the children, which would have caused Juan to have no decision-making power as it related to the children. Although her desire went unfulfilled, she agreed to abide by the judge's decision.

For a while, both parents worked together to stay on schedule and from time to time, each one requested changes, and the other attempted to be accommodating as much as possible. But then, things changed for the worse. Seemingly, out of nowhere, Marisol's temper flared up, and she began changing the visitation schedule without notice. Juan would go to pick the children up, and they would be unavailable. That caused fury to grow within him.

As more time passed, Juan felt he was slowly losing his children, as it would be weeks in between the times he saw them rather than seeing them on the weekly schedule set by the judge. His patience was wearing thin- both with Marisol and the court system. No matter how much he complained, he received a deaf ear from both. He did not understand how Marisol could deny him the opportunity to care, bond, nurture, and interact with his children. From his perspective, there were too many absentee fathers, and he had no intention of adding to the count. He was certain Marisol would appreciate that about him. Unfortunately, things did not appear that way.

Eventually, Juan knew he had to deal with matters with a firmer hand. So, on one unfortunate occasion when his children were not available for pick up when they should have been, he called the local authorities and reported the infraction. An officer took his information down and instructed him to contact the court. Juan followed the officer's instructions. How-ever, the court failed to offer much assistance. Needless to say, Juan had hit a road block.

A few months later, things took a turn for the worse. Not only was the set visitation schedule not being adhered to on a continual basis, it seemed to have had completely evaporated. Juan didn't see his children at all, and Marisol had stopped taking his calls. When he drove to the house in which they lived, they were never there. That was devastating for Juan. So, back to the authorities he went. Again, he was referred to the court. Reluctantly, he went to the court, and once again he filled out the proper forms. That time, he received a hearing date, which led back to mediation.

After months and months of battling with Marisol in court, Juan fought to have the custody order changed. In his favor, he became the custodial parent, and Marisol was granted supervised visitation as a result of her previous conduct of withholding the children. From that point forward, the children led more stable lives, and Juan had peace of mind.

Marisol was not the happiest of them all, but her actions had led to those particular consequences. It was a long and arduous road to travel, but Juan loved his children from the depths of his soul, and he would fight to the death to remain a constant figure in their lives. He never wanted them to grow up fatherless, and he would always do everything in his power to ensure that did not happen.

Tracy

By the time Tracy had reached thirty-four years of age, she had been in and out of relationships, not being able to stay in one for more than a year. She desired to get married, but no one had ever proposed. In most of her relationships, the guy had broken up with her, stating she was too needy and/or too clingy. Tracy did not understand why they would make such a big deal when she would call them continuously throughout the day or because she wanted to know their whereabouts or she constantly wanted to be in their presence when both of them were off work. She viewed her desire to be close as a regular part of a relationship, but the men felt smothered.

After dating several "bad apples," as Tracy referred to them, she met Ryan. After dating for a year and a half and surpassing the normal timeline of her past relationships, Tracy grew hopeful that she and Ryan would be heading to the altar soon. He had never brought up the subject of marriage, but little by little, Tracy began to introduce marriage into their conversations to see how Ryan felt about it. She even went as far as having dinner parties and inviting married couples to join them when normally it would be a group of single people hanging out and having a great time.

After a few months of coaxing, Ryan warmed up to the idea of them exchanging vows and having a life-long relationship together. However, Ryan was not as anxious as Tracy was to head to the altar. Rather than make a decision he did not believe either one was ready for, he suggested they move in together to see how well they functioned as a couple who lived under the same roof. Although Tracy did not believe in couples living together before marriage, she felt she was not getting any younger and needed to do what was necessary to solidify her relationship with Ryan. She did not want to endure another breakup, so she relented.

A few months after Ryan suggested they move in together, they went apartment hunting and found one they both found comfortable. It was conveniently located between their two jobs and was affordable for both of their budgets. They split the rent and all expenses in half, each sharing an equal amount of the financial responsibility. Although Tracy agreed when Ryan suggested splitting the expenses, secretly she believed he should shoulder the responsibility as he was the man. She reminded herself he was not her husband and therefore let the issue rest.

Eight months went by, and Tracy and Ryan seemed to be really settling in as a cohabitating couple. Their conversations were jovial and when issues arose, they were able to discuss them and settle them amicably. They even began to spend time with each other's family on a regular basis. Everyone knew them as a couple.

Also, things were improving for Ryan at work. He had taken a promotion and was given a higher salary, but he was required to work longer hours and even some weekends. From time to time, he had to go on business trips with his boss, as he was the executive assistant. Occasionally, he would ask Tracy to travel with him, but due to her own work schedule, most times she was unable to go. As a result, Tracy constantly complained about Ryan's changing work schedule and began to accuse him of having an affair when their time together grew limited.

Ryan was bothered by Tracy's immature attitude and her accusations, especially when she knew the truth. There was nothing in his behavior to cause her to suspect him of cheating. She had access to him at work and could stop by at will. Nevertheless, her insecurities got the best of her. He thought the best way to put her mind at ease was to demonstrate how loyal and serious he was about her and their relationship, so he proposed. Tracy accepted his proposal but was further agitated and began to distance herself when Ryan refused to set a date for the wedding.

As time drew on, Ryan decided the relationship and the stress that came with it was causing too much harm to his job because he was unable to focus the way he needed.

He began to suffer from headaches and anxiety. Never in his life had a relationship been that much work. He did not understand it, and he was convinced he was working overtime on his and Tracy's relationship - unnecessarily.

After trying to talk to Tracy about her disposition on several occasions, Ryan decided it would be best to end their relationship because Tracy was obstinate and unwilling to alter her mindset or disposition as it related to her behavior, accusations, and Ryan's professional life.

His change of heart shocked Tracy into reality. But, it was much too late. She had not realized her behavior was having such a devastating effect on them. She thought she was simply voicing her opinion about what she believed was occurring. Obviously, Ryan saw it completely differently. As Tracy and Ryan discussed the break up, they discussed who would be moving out of the apartment. They both admitted they could not afford to pay for an apartment on their own with their present income and retain the same type of lifestyle they had been accustomed to living. Ryan's new salary had just gone into effect, so he wanted stability before taking on a full load of responsibilities on his own.

Prior to moving in together, Tracy had a roommate in another apartment. Ryan, on the other hand, was living with his brother and his family. Tracy's prior roommate had found another roommate, so she could not move back in with her. Ryan did not want to impose upon his brother and his family again, so they decided to remain in their apartment for the next five months until the lease was up. Then, they would decide how to proceed from there. More than likely, Ryan would stay in that apartment, and Tracy would find one that was less expensive, so she could manage on her own.

With that arrangement, Ryan moved from the master bedroom into the spare bedroom. They had been using the spare bedroom as a shared office space. After the new arrangement began, each set up an office inside their own bedroom.

Tracy was completely heartbroken and could not figure out where she had gone wrong. But, hope prevailed! Tracy believed she and Ryan had a chance to work it out while they were under the same roof. Her plan was not to bother him, stressing him out. She would be sweet and take things slowly. She believed over time, they could mend their relationship and pick up where they had left off before things got out of control.

Ryan, on the other hand, was done with the relationship. He had no intention of mending it. He was looking forward to finding an apartment and moving out once the lease expired, if Tracy refused to move. To make his point clear, he would leave his laptop on the kitchen counter with websites of apartment searches in the browser history. He knew Tracy would look through his belongings, probably searching for evidence of another woman. She had been doing that since they moved in together. He had been aware of it but had chosen not to say anything. He had nothing to hide, and he figured sooner or later, Tracy would know the truth about him.

When Tracy saw evidence of Ryan searching for apartments, she grew depressed from disappointment. She had been cooking Ryan special dinners of his favorite foods, and from time to time, they would sleep together in each other's room. Ryan knew it was not wise to lead Tracy on. He did care about her, even though he did not see a future with her. To him, their activity was just them keeping each other company. For her, there was hope that the separation could be mended.

When Ryan noticed Tracy was acting as if they were a couple again, he decided it would be best to keep his distance and not engage with her too much. He began calling her "roomy," instead of using terms of endearment. He realized the feelings she had for him were still strong and had not begun to decrease as his had. About a month later, after he stopped spending time in her room, he started dating. He knew it would not be best to bring dates to the apartment, so when necessary, he would go to his date's home to be alone.

One night when Ryan did not come home, Tracy called his phone incessantly as if though he was her husband who was staying away from his wife and children. She called his phone so many times, he had to turn it off just to get some peace and not disturb his date. When Ryan returned home from work the next evening, he was confronted by Tracy as soon as he walked in the door. Not only was she verbally abusive, but she became physically confrontational as well.

After the same episode repeated itself twice more, Ryan decided it would be best to move out immediately, even if it meant paying rent at two different locations. When Ryan entered the apartment one Saturday afternoon with moving boxes, Tracy began crying hysterically. Ryan did not know what to do. He called Cynthia, a friend of Tracy's, to come over to console her. Cynthia helped Tracy pack an overnight bag and took her to her home.

The next day was Sunday, and Cynthia was an avid church goer. She invited Tracy to go with her to the morning worship service. Tracy had a hard time getting out of bed, and she really did not want to go, but she felt a change of pace may do her some good. Plus, she enjoyed worship service. She had been avoiding going because she believed she was out of God's will.

During the service, Tracy fidgeted in her seat as the minister shared the message for the day. Several times, Cynthia placed a gentle hand on Tracy's leg to calm her nervous mannerisms. Once Tracy was calm, she was able to listen to the message. She heard the minister say, "Do not allow the enemy to steal your joy! That is not the will of God. Jesus said in John 14:27, *'Peace I leave with you, my peace I give unto you: not as the world giveth, give I unto you. Let not your heart be troubled, neither let it be afraid.'* So, use the authority that God has given you and take control over your life. The enemy wants to come in and confuse you, to make you believe you are not worthy of love. God loves you. You do not need someone else's love to validate you. The enemy will make you feel as though you are nothing, but you are precious to God. Don't you understand, He made you a little lower than the angels (Psalm 8:5)."

Tracy left the worship service feeling tremendously better than she had when she had entered the sanctuary. However, it did not take her long to fall back into her regular pattern of low self-esteem, believing she needed someone to love her in order for her to be valuable. Cynthia noticed the stronghold the enemy had on Tracy. So, she began to pick her up each week to take her to church.

Meanwhile, Ryan moved out. His absence was extremely difficult for Tracy, but it was in their best interest to make a clean break without being in each other's presence each day. For weeks, Tracy called Ryan with the pretense of checking on him as friends, but she actually was trying to keep tabs on him and his whereabouts. Sometimes, he would answer her call, and other times he would not. Not hearing from Ryan drove Tracy crazy.

Tracy's pattern of destruction continued for some time. In an effort to help, Cynthia obtained a copy of the minister's message on CD that was preached the first Sunday Tracy had attended and gave it to Tracy. Tracy played the CD in her car over and over again. Also, Cynthia and Tracy began to fellowship with other singles in the church, going on outings and enjoying each other's company.

It took almost a full year for Tracy to turn the metaphorical corner in her level of self-esteem. She began to have more confidence in herself, without having a man on her arm to boost her ego. She began to value herself and allow the Lord to give her a makeover, starting from the inside first. Tracy understood she was a work in progress, but she was adamant about standing her ground and taking back all the enemy had stolen from her. She refused to be another statistic, another victim. She was determined to be another victor because He had made her more than a conqueror (Romans 8:37), and she believed His Word.

Two years later, Tracy was hosting seminars and workshops, sharing her story with other women and men. After all she had been through, she wanted to share her story to encourage others. After all, isn't that what trials and tests are for? If you can endure them to the end and come out a victor, you should be able to share with someone. Revelation 12:11 says, *"And they overcame him by the blood of the Lamb, and by the word of their testimony; and they loved not their lives unto the death."* When we share our testimonies, we overcome the strategies and wiles of the enemy.

The enemy wants to weaken our resolve, but we are strong and mighty through the power of the Lord. Tracy was able to break free from the enemy's stronghold, and you have the same power and authority. Exercise it!

Stand...

"Wherefore take unto you the whole armour of God, that ye may be able to withstand in the evil day, and having done all, to stand. Stand therefore, having your loins girt about with truth, and having on the breastplate of righteousness; And your feet shod with the preparation of the gospel of peace; Above all, taking the shield of faith, wherewith ye shall be able to quench all the fiery darts of the wicked. And take the helmet of salvation, and the sword of the Spirit, which is the word of God: Praying always with all prayer and supplication in the Spirit, and watching thereunto with all perseverance and supplication for all saints."
Ephesians 6:13-18

After reading the accounts of the daughters of Zelophehad and their determination to obtain their land inheritance, Brigit and the troubles she endured with her husband's adult children when he willed her a home and a portion of his wealth, Luci's trial with obtaining her pension, Marisol and Juan's child custody battle, Tracy and her journey to overcome low self-esteem, and Rani and her seven-month escapade of reclaiming stolen family heirlooms, we have many examples of the types of trials we could face during our lifetime. And, none of us who traverse God's green earth is exempt from trials of any magnitude or of any form.

On the other side of the learning curve, we learn no matter the trial we face, we will need determination to see the trial through to the end. Determination will assist us in standing our ground, so we can fight for what is rightfully ours. Coupled with determination, believers have the Word of God as a foundation, providing solid footing on which to balance in times of distress.

Ask yourself the following questions: Will you always be strong, possessing the strength to walk through the trial? Will you always feel like persevering and finding the correct path without giving up mid-stream? Will you always have unconditional support from loved ones, family, and friends? Will you always have emotional and mental stability? The obvious answer to these four questions and others similar to it, although we may proport otherwise, is no.

When we are weak, the Lord is our strength. *"God is our refuge and strength, a very present help in trouble. Therefore will not we fear, though the earth be removed, and though the mountains be carried into the midst of the sea; Though the waters thereof roar and be troubled, though the mountains shake with the swelling thereof. Selah"* (Psalm 46:1-3). *"Then he said unto them, Go your way, eat the fat, and drink the sweet, and send portions unto them for whom nothing is prepared: for this day is holy unto our Lord: neither be ye sorry; for the joy of the Lord is your strength"* (Nehemiah 8:10).

When we do not have the will to persevere, God is the one who will make a way for us when we cannot carve out one for ourselves and when we cannot find the correct path on which to travel. Isaiah 43:16-19 informs us: *"Thus saith the Lord, which maketh a way in the sea, and a path in the mighty waters; Which bringeth forth the chariot and horse, the army and the power; they shall lie down together, they shall not rise: they are extinct, they are quenched as tow. Remember ye not the former things, neither consider the things of old. Behold, I will do a new thing; now it shall spring forth; shall ye not know it? I will even make a way in the wilderness, and rivers in the desert."*

When no one cares enough to understand what we are dealing with or are unable to assist, the all-knowing god, Jehovah, will be there with us every step of the journey, and He will make the proper provisions. Psalm 46:8-11 says, *"Come, behold the works of the Lord, what desolations he hath made in the earth. He maketh wars to cease unto the end of the earth; he breaketh the bow, and cutteth the spear in sunder; he burneth the chariot in the fire. Be still, and know that I am God: I will be exalted among the heathen, I will be exalted in the earth. The Lord of hosts is with us; the God of Jacob is our refuge. Selah."*

Psalm 18:6-19 says, *"In my distress I called upon the Lord, and cried unto my God: he heard my voice out of his temple, and my cry came before him, even into his ears. Then the earth shook and trembled; the foundations also of the hills moved and were shaken, because he was wroth. There went up a smoke out of his nostrils, and fire out of his mouth devoured: coals were kindled by it. He bowed the heavens also, and came down: and darkness was under his feet. And he rode upon a cherub, and did fly: yea, he did fly upon the wings of the wind. He made darkness his secret place; his pavilion round about him were dark waters and thick clouds of the skies. At the brightness that was before him his thick clouds passed, hail stones and coals of fire. The Lord also thundered in the heavens, and the Highest gave his voice; hail stones and coals of fire. Yea, he sent out his arrows, and scattered them; and he shot out lightnings, and discomfited them. Then the channels of waters were seen, and the foundations of the world were discovered at thy rebuke, O Lord, at the blast of the breath of thy nostrils. He sent from above, he took me, he drew me out of many waters. He delivered me from my strong enemy, and from them which hated me: for they were too strong for me. They prevented me in the day of my calamity: but the Lord was my stay. He brought me forth also into a large place; he delivered me, because he delighted in me."*

Psalm 91:14-16 says, *"Because he hath set his love upon me, therefore will I deliver him: I will set him on high, because he hath known my name. He shall call upon me, and I will answer him: I will be with him in trouble; I will deliver him, and honour him. With long life will I satisfy him, and shew him my salvation."*

Hebrews 4:14-16 says, *"Seeing then that we have a great high priest, that is passed into the heavens, Jesus the Son of God, let us hold fast our profession. For we have not an high priest which cannot be touched with the feeling of our infirmities; but was in all points tempted like as we are, yet without sin. Let us therefore come boldly unto the throne of grace, that we may obtain mercy, and find grace to help in time of need."*

When our emotions and thoughts are erratic and uncontrollable, we should turn to the Word of God for comfort, knowing God wants the best for us. His desire is for us to flourish and prosper, so He provides His providence for our benefit. Philippians 4:7 states, *"And the peace of God, which passeth all under-standing, shall keep your hearts and minds through Christ Jesus."* Proverbs 16:32 shares, *"He that is slow to anger is better than the mighty; and he that ruleth his spirit than he that taketh a city."*

Colossians 3:2 says, *"Set your affection on things above, not on things on the earth."* Romans 8:6 states, *"For to be carnally minded is death; but to be spiritually minded is life and peace."* II Corinthians 5:7 declares, *"For we walk by faith, not by sight."* Proverbs 3:5-6 states, *"Trust in the Lord with all thine heart; and lean not unto thine own understanding. In all thy ways acknowledge him, and he shall direct thy paths."*

No matter the trials we face, and no matter if we have an earthly shoulder to lean on, God's Word is our foundation, and God Himself is our shoulder, for He is our strong tower. He is mighty in battle and shall never be defeated! To get through any trial, we must remember who we are in Him and the power He has given us. We are more than conquerors, and in Him, and we can do anything but fail!

Gift of Salvation for Non-Believers

"For all have sinned, and come short of the glory of God."
*(*Romans 3:23)

This section was written especially for non-believers, those who have not accepted the gift of salvation. The gift of salvation saves souls from eternal damnation and is a free gift offered by God himself.

John 3:16-18 says, "*For God so loved the world, that he gave his only begotten Son, that whosoever believeth in him should not perish, but have everlasting life. For God sent not his Son into the world to condemn the world; but that the world through him might be saved. He that believeth on him is not condemned: but he that believeth not is condemned already, because he hath not believed in the name of the only begotten Son of God.*"

This section of scripture tells us God's purpose for giving His son Jesus to the world. The world was in a bad condition. The world was overwrought with sin; the people were living for fleshly desires rather than for God's desires.

As a result of the world's conditions, God decided He would offer the perfect sacrifice that would save the world from being a place where people were lost and had no hope. He decided that His own son could stand in proxy for the sin-filled world, taking all sin upon Himself.

So Jesus came, born of a virgin, to save this dying world. He walked on this earth for 33 ½ years, doing the work of His Heavenly Father. At the appointed time, He died by way of crucifixion upon a cross at Calvary, on Golgatha's hill. He shed his blood and died for you and for me. Because His blood was pure, it paid the penalty for all unrighteousness and gave those who believe in Him direct access to His father's throne.

Scripture tells us in Matthew 27:51 that the veil of the temple was ripped in two from top to bottom, at the moment that Jesus' spirit left His body. As a result of the veil's removal, we are no longer required to have a high priest make intercession for us. We, as the children of the Most High God, are able to approach the throne God for ourselves, and Jesus sits on the right hand of the Father making intercession for us.

But what is even more miraculous than God offering His own son as the perfect sacrifice was the fact that when Jesus was placed in grave clothes and placed in a tomb, He only remained there until the third day. God would not have it that His son would remain in the heart of the earth forever. In order for people to believe in the awesome power of God and His dear son Jesus, a miracle had to be performed. So, on the third day, after Jesus died on the cross, He was resurrected, demonstrating the omnipotence of God. This very act was the act that would cause people to believe in a god that reigns supreme and holds the power of the universe in His very hands, a god that could save them from themselves.

Today, if you are an unbeliever, you can change your destiny. You can change where you will spend your eternity. Our Heavenly Father gives us the freedom of choice about how we want to live our life here on earth and how we want to spend eternity. In Deuteronomy 30:19, God boldly declares, "*I call heaven and earth to record this day against you, that I have set before you life and death, blessing and cursing: therefore choose life, that both thou and thy seed may live.*"

So, dear friend what choice will you make today? Will you spend your eternity with the Creator or will you suffer Hell's eternal flames? Again, the choice is yours. Just as the men aboard the ship who were with Jonah became believers, you too can make a choice to accept the only one and true living God as your god.

If after reading the above passages, you have decided that you want to spend your eternity in Heaven with God, the creator, and His son Jesus, and the Holy Spirit, read through what has affectionately come to be known as the Roman's Road. This is the road to salvation. As you read through the scriptures that comprise the Roman's Road, you will also read the explanation for each scripture so you will have clarity about what you are reading and confessing.

The Roman's Road to Salvation

The road to salvation begins with Romans 3:23 which declares, "*For all have sinned, and come short of the glory of God.*" This scripture explains that everyone has come short of God's glory and needs redemption. Then Romans 6:23a states, "*For the wages of sin is death.*" Here, we learn that the consequence of living a life of sin is death. Everyone will experience physical death as a result of the sin committed in the garden of Eden, but those who commit themselves to a life of sin will suffer eternal damnation in the lake of fire (Rev. 19).

Continue with the rest of verse 6:23 that says, *"but the gift of God is eternal life through Jesus Christ our Lord."* There is an alternative to suffering eternal damnation. We can accept the gift of salvation by accepting Jesus as our personal lord and savior. Then, Romans 5:8 says, *"But God commendeth his love toward us, in that, while we were yet sinners, Christ died for us."* We are able to receive the gift of salvation because Christ came to earth and shed His blood for us on the cross.

Continue to Romans 10: 9-10 which says, *"That if thou shalt confess with thy mouth the Lord Jesus, and shalt believe in thine heart that God hath raised him from the dead, thou shalt be saved. For with the heart man believeth unto righteousness; and with the mouth confession is made unto salvation."* If we confess with our mouths that Jesus is the son of God, that he came and died for our sins, and that God raised Him from the dead, we will receive salvation.

Finish with Romans 10:13, which states, *"For whosoever shall call upon the name of the Lord shall be saved."* Call upon the name of God by saying these words, **"Lord Jesus, come into my heart and save me Lord. I believe that you are the Son of God who came and died on the cross for my sins. I believe that you rose from the grave. I also believe that you now sit in heaven on the right side of the Father, making intersession for me. I accept you as my Lord and my Savior.**"

Now that you have confessed with your mouth that Jesus is the son of God and that He died for our sins and rose from the grave, **YOU ARE NOW SAVED!!!!** You will spend your eternity in heaven.

The next step is very important- you must find a Bible-based church that teaches the word of God and confesses the Lord Jesus Christ to be the son of God. Don't delay. Do this immediately. Do not leave yourself open to the enemy. Get connected with the saints of the Most High God and keep yourself covered with the unspotted blood of the lamb. Here is my prayer for you.

Father God,

I thank you for the opportunity to minister your word to the unsaved, the unchurched, and the uncommitted. Father God, I pray now for the souls who have just received the gift of salvation. Lord Father, they have opened their hearts to you, and I know that you have received them into your kingdom and written their names in the Book of Life. Father God, I pray that you will touch their lives and show yourself mightily before them. Let their eyes be opened by the scales falling off, allowing them to see clearly.

Father God, I even pray for the backslider, those who have turned away from you after receiving the gift of salvation. You said in your word that you desire that none would perish. So Lord, I send your word to them right now praying that they would confess the iniquity in their heart, repent, and turn from their evil ways, so that they may receive a life of abundance. You said in your word in Matthew Chapter 14, that every knee shall bow before you and every tongue will confess that Jesus is Lord.

Father God, I pray now that we all come under subjection to your word and that we will humbly submit our lives to you. I ask all these things in the name of my Lord and Savior Jesus Christ.

Amen, Amen, Amen!!!!

I will continue to pray for your success in your walk with God. Remember, this spiritual walk that you are about to embark on will not be an easy walk, but remember, the race is not given to the swift but to those who endure to the end.

Be blessed with heaven's best. I love you!

OTHER BOOKS BY THE AUTHOR

(All books can be purchased at amazon.com, barnesandnoble.com and www.creativemindsbookstore.com)

From Despair, through Determination, to Victory!

A lot can happen during a span of 40 years. The life of Dr. Cassundra White-Elliott has been anything but uneventful. From a fun-loving childhood sprinkled with incidents of abuse to a tumultuous young adulthood to a stable, secure adult life, she has experienced a full life, with much more to come. Her story is inspiring and motivating.

If anyone lacks hope, reading Dr. White-Elliott's autobiography will propel him/her into an attitude of "Maybe I can." This attitude, if nurtured and developed, will grow into an attitude of "Yes, I can." Throughout her life, Cassundra has always held in her heart the belief that she could achieve anything that she had a made-up mind to embark upon. She was determined to achieve her heart's desires, doing what God has called her to do. She takes no credit for herself. All the glory goes to God, for He is her driving force. In Him, she lives, moves, and has her being.

Through the Storm

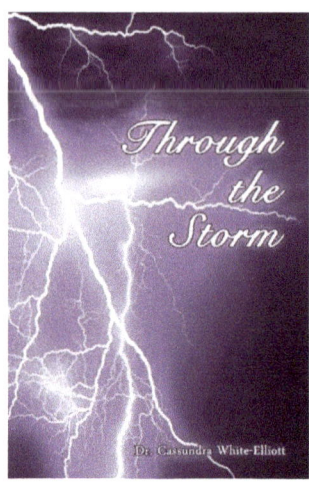

Through the Storm was duly inspired by the avaricious cloud of depression that decided to hover overhead of my daily existence in the latter part of 2007. Although I found it extremely difficult, I was once again compelled to not be defeated by just another snare that the enemy, the trickster, set for me. Once again, or more appropriately I should say *continuously*, he has exerted pernicious efforts to snatch the very life out of me by causing me to wallow in despair and to believe that I had been overcome by failure when in actuality and all reality, I was just experiencing a temporary setback. During those cloudy days, I had to remind myself daily that even though I was a target of the enemy, I am and will always be a child of the Most High God, Jehovah, who is my rock, my stability.

Unleashed Anger, Anger Unleashed

Introduction
What Is This Book All About?

As I prepared to embark upon the adventure of writing this book, I had to prepare myself to also be transparent. I have found that being transparent is required in order for healing to transpire, healing for all those that peruse the pages of this book and myself. And I may as well tell you that today, at the onset of this project, I have not been totally delivered from my condition of being an anger-filled person. However, I am definitely a work in progress. I have made strides with the assistance of my Lord and Savior, Jesus Christ, who is the head of my life. Without his love, guidance, and teachings, I would not be the woman of God I am today. I shudder to think where I could be instead and will therefore not entertain the thought.

Public Speaking in the Spiritual Arena

Chapter Two
How Communication Works
Purpose: This chapter will explain the six primary components of communication, identifying their purpose and how they work together.

The Source

In oral communication, the source of information is the speaker. In a church setting, the foundation of the message is God's word, but it is a speaker's interpretation of God's word that is delivered to the audience. As speakers vary, the information may vary but should have a similar essence because the foundational text is the same.

The Message

The message is the collective set of ideas that the speaker (the source) wants to deliver and/or illustrate to the audience. The message can be informative where the speaker informs the audience about a specific set of information. Or, the message may be persuasive in nature if the speaker wants to persuade the audience about conducting themselves in a specific manner, accepting God's commandments, or any number of things.

Where is Your Joppa?

Introduction

Where is Your Joppa? was written for the express purpose of illustrating God's call for obedience in the lives of believers with respect to the individual call that He has on each of our lives. As you read throughout the various chapters, notice that the emphasis is placed on our persistent disobedience in answering God's call in a specific area of our lives. We have become a people who are similar to the Israelites when they found themselves in the middle of the wilderness, following their exodus from Egypt. Before God, they murmured and complained about their current life conditions and failed to be obedient to God's statutes delivered through His servant Moses. Their persistent disobedience caused them to lose the opportunity to see and enter the Promised Land. I ask you, "What has your disobedience cost you?" "Was your disobedience worth what it cost you?" "Do you think about the souls you could have ushered into the kingdom of God?" These are some of the questions that I pray will be answered through your reading of the book.

Mayhem in the Hamptons

Romero and Yolanda optimistically plan for the day that is going to change their lives from being single persons to a couple who is united in holy matrimony. They, along with their parents, close friends and family, fly over to the infamous Hamptons, where only the rich and famous vacation, to have their dream wedding at the five-star Hampton Suites located on a peninsula in the Hamptons. Little do they know that their perfect day will turn out to be less than perfect when their wedding planner Mariesha Coleman suddenly goes missing!

A time when the newlyweds' lives should be filled with joy and the creation of wonderful memories, they are stricken with grief as they desperately try to find clues to help solve Mariesha's disappearance.

Mayhem in the Hamptons is a tale that shares how the horrors of a woman's past can come back to haunt her in more than one way and the impact it can have on anyone who gets in the way.

Preacher's Daughter

Tinisha, the daughter of a preacher, is a twenty-six year old God-fearing young woman endeavoring to complete law school so that she can make her mark in the courtroom. Working in one of the late-night clubs in Hollywood to earn money to pay her own way through school, Tinisha soon learns that life doesn't always go as planned. Finding her strength in her faith, Tinisha constantly finds herself praying as she watches God move miraculously in her life.

Preacher's Son

Romero Turner is a private investigator with a promising future. As he continues to build his career, he is excited about the cases he undertakes. However, his father Pastor Theodore Turner has other plans for his son's life. In the midst of trying to save his client's husband from Sylvester Domingo, a ruthless crime lord, Romero must try to salvage his relationship with his father. He must decide if ministry or life as a detective is in his future.

Lord, Teach Me to be a Blessing!

Lord, Teach Me to be a Blessing! will change a person's mentality from being centered around "me, myself, and I" to focusing on "others."

The world system teaches us that it is acceptable to place ourselves above others in an attempt to get ahead and even to survive. Herbert Spencer coined the phrase '*survival of the fittest*' after reading Charles Darwin's theory of evolution. This concept of surpassing and outdoing others is the world's philosophy.

However, the word of God does not subscribe to or promote this self-centered ideology, and therefore, neither should believers. We must hold fast to the truths outlined in Holy Scripture: "*Love thy neighbor as you love thyself*" (James 2:8) and "*It is more blessed to give than to receive*" (Acts 20:35).

While holding God's truths to be self-evident, we must demonstrate them to others, thereby showing them the way of the Lord of how to be a blessing to someone *rather* than looking to receive a blessing.

After the Dust Settles

Throughout the journey of life, we all experience ups and downs and joys and pains. Most of us successfully find solutions to the situations/problems we encounter, but we often avoid dealing with the attached emotions. If we continue to ignore the emotions of pain, hurt, disappointment, anger, etc., we set ourselves up for destruction. Our families, our cultures, and our society tell us to be strong, to keep our chin up, and to grin and bear it. However, these methods of avoidance can lead us to strokes due to the undue amount of pressure we place on ourselves and/or mental illness from being unable to cope with the emotional baggage we have accumulated.

In *After the Dust Settles,* Dr. C. White-Elliott shares several situations that we all may encounter at one time or another in our lifetime and how to successfully navigate through them, so we can find ourselves emotionally healthy after the dust has settled and the situation has been rectified.

Begin reading today and experience a better tomorrow!

A Diamond in the Rough

A Diamond in the Rough Architecture Firm was built and is owned and operated by lead architect Kyra Fraser. For the last five years, Kyra has been extremely successful in business, but her love life leaves much to be desired.

Kyra has set high standards for herself and does not wish to take a man in any condition and attempt to make him over. She is looking for someone who is drama free, well educated, very cultured, fun-loving, good looking, self-motivated, and the list goes on.

Will Kyra find the man of her dreams, or will her dream just continue to be a dream?

As you delve into this page-turning novel, Kyra's reality will unfold as you are drawn into her world of design, love and office drama- which includes her best friend's husband who is looking for love in all the wrong places.

365 Days of Encouragement

Just as our brain requires oxygen obtained from the air we breathe to sustain our mortal bodies, our spirit requires revitalization and encouragement in order to be strengthened each and every day of our lives. The revitalization and encouragement needed for the spirit of man comes directly from the word of God and assists us in walking according to the way of our heavenly Father. 365 Days of Encouragement provides a scripture a day for each day of the year. Along with the daily scripture is a brief note of commentary also for the benefit of edifying the saints of God.

It is my prayer that the people of God would live a fulfilled life through Christ Jesus. Knowing His word and understanding we can walk in the fulfillment thereof is empowering. We are instructed in II Timothy 2:15, "Study to shew thyself approved unto God, a workman that needeth not to be ashamed, rightly dividing the word of truth" (KJV). Take an opportunity to delve further into the word of God, to know His statutes and to allow your own personal life to be edified, so you can be equipped to bring glory to God and lived a fulfilled life.

A Mother's Heart

A Mother's Heart shares the unconditional love of mothers through a compilation of testimonies. Each testimony serves as a tribute to a special mother. The children of the represented mothers have lovingly written about their childhood, young adult life and/or older adult experiences they shared with their mother. As you read the writers' reflections, you will feel the expressions of love exude from the pages.

The purpose of this book is two-fold. First, it honors those mothers who stood by their children through the trials of life and showered them with unconditional love. Second, the book is a source of encouragement for mothers who may feel inadequate and question whether or not they are actually suited for motherhood. Our advice to mothers is, "Be encouraged; the journey of motherhood may seem daunting at times and you may shed some tears, but your children will never forget the love you have shown them and instilled in them to share with others."

Mothers may not be perfect, but they are definitely unmatched by any other category of person on God's green earth!

Broken Chains

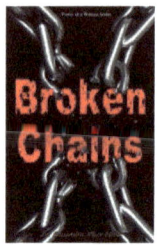

Broken Chains is an in-depth survey of five life-changing tragedies that can and will serve as chains to bind us if we are not watchful and mindful of their potential effects. In our lifetimes, we may all experience death of loved ones, sexual abuse, broken relationships, promiscuity, and sickness and disease. These everyday life occurrences can have detrimental effects on the remaining years of our lives and change our existence, unless we deal with them in a healthy manner.

Broken Chains not only brings to light the detrimental effects of five life-changing tragedies, but it also shares how anyone who experiences them can be healed and delivered from their effects.

If you have experienced death of a loved one, sexual abuse, a broken relationship, the effects of promiscuity, and/or sickness and disease and have not been able to rid yourself of the emotions attached to them or specific resulting behaviors, Broken Chains is for you.

God designed each of us for a purpose, and He has an intended end for us to achieve. In order for us to effectively achieve our God-given purpose, we must be free of chains that bind us. It is not God's desire that we become immobilized by life's events. His desire is for us to be healed, delivered and set free. Be healed today, in the name of the Lord Jesus Christ!

I Have Fallen

Do you know anyone who has committed his/her life to Christ but has done something unseemly that you would never expect a Christian to do? How did you feel about that person or what the person did? Did you pass judgment? What if that person were you? How would you feel if you made a misstep and no one forgave you and instead began to treat you differently? How do you feel when you are judged for past mistakes or lifestyles that are no longer part of your life?

This book shares four true stories of Christians who have made missteps during their walk with God. The purpose is not to air their dirty laundry, but to demonstrate our humanness and our vulnerability. None of us are exempt from making errors and falling into sin. It can happen to any of us.

The solution for these dilemmas is for the person who fell into sin to make a life-changing move and turn away from the sin, repent and ask God for forgiveness. His arms are waiting!

The next solution is for those who witness the sin or know of it. Pray and be of comfort to the one who has fallen. Lead him/her back to the path of righteousness. Love thy neighbor and treat him/her as you want to be treated!

The Bottom Line

The Bottom Line is a detailed review of the Book of Job. Much can be said about Job's experiences with the loss of his children and wealth and the subsequent return of it all in mass proportions. However, the telling of Job's story in the Holy writ was not intended to focus on the return of his wealth. Instead, the focal point should be on the bottom line of the entire situation.

When you experience trials or tragedies in your life, do you tend to focus on the trial itself, the result, or the bottom line?

"What is the bottom line?" you may ask. The bottom line is the message God is sending regarding the situation.

When Job experienced his tragedies, there was a bottom line. Likewise, when you experience your trials and tragedies, there is a bottom line as well. It is up to you to discover it.

This book will reveal the bottom line in the Book of Job. It is readily apparent, but many often overlook it.

Now, it is up to you to uncover the bottom line of your experiences, for God will not bring a trial to you without a good reason.

Power of a Woman

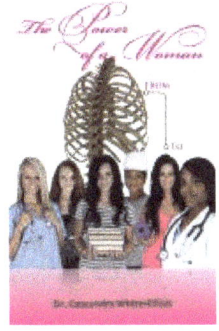

The ongoing conversation about the value of a woman is presented from a different perspective in The Power of a Woman. Dr. Cassundra White-Elliott presents a biblical perspective of women and compares it to the worldview of both yesterday and today. This comparison seeks to illustrate God's intended purpose for His uniquely designed creation: woman. Dr. Elliott shares God's truth about pre-imposed limitations set by man versus the limitations God Himself set for woman in addition to the wealth of liberality He gave her.

Women's creativity and abilities are not meant to be stifled. They are meant to be utilized to bring glory to God, to help sustain and nurture their families, and to move the world forward. Knowing God's truth will show women how to celebrate and appreciate who they are as well as one another!

Women, let's take the blinders off, lift our heads up, and march forward, side by side with men, and bring glory and honor to God! Take your rightful place with a gentle smile and grace and be who God called you to be!

Set Free

If you possess habits and display characteristics that are unbecoming, debilitating, and hinder the desired progress in your life or that affect your relationships with others, Set Free will provide the steps you need to be healed and delivered, through the Word of God.

Deliverance is available to you! Claim your healing today and walk in victory!

Do You Know God?

Have you or someone you know ever felt alone, confused, or unsure about your walk with God or are you unsure of what being a Christian is all about? *Do You Know God?* is an excellent text for providing answers to many of your questions. This book introduces adolescents and young adults to God in addition to answer many of their questions about being a Christian. This book shares the testimonies of the trials and tribulations that other teens have experienced and how God prevailed in their lives. All the information that is shared on the pages of the book is based upon the Word of God and the scriptures are taken from the King James Version of the Bible. If you are interested in knowing more about God's Word or how to begin your Christian experience, this book is for you.

Web of Lies

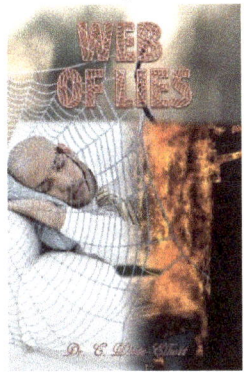

A year ago, Charlito Jimenez was found in his den, lying on the couch, with a fatal gunshot wound in his temple. Everyone in the community still wants to know who is guilty of the unfathomable crime.

Tinisha Salisbury, attorney at law, has taken the case of the accused. Can she prove her client's innocence or will a guilty verdict be rendered?

Halfway through the trial, a badly burned body was found at the scene of a fire.

Is there a string of murders being committed?

Are the murders related?

Web of Lies spins the tales of several characters into one web. Each has a story to tell, and everyone has something to hide. The web of lies, deceit, and revenge take over the lives of these characters to the point where they may not be able to see their way clear.

www.ingramcontent.com/pod-product-compliance
Lightning Source LLC
LaVergne TN
LVHW070013090426
835508LV00048B/3382